SWEAR WORD COLORING BOOK For Adults

A Fucking Motivating And Sweary But Stress Relieving One

Hardcore Edition

By Fun In Color

Copyright
© 2019 Fun In Color

All rights reserved. This book or any portion thereof may not be reproduced or used in any manner whatsoever without the express written permission of the publisher except for the use of brief quotations in a book review.

First printing, 2019.

SAMPLES

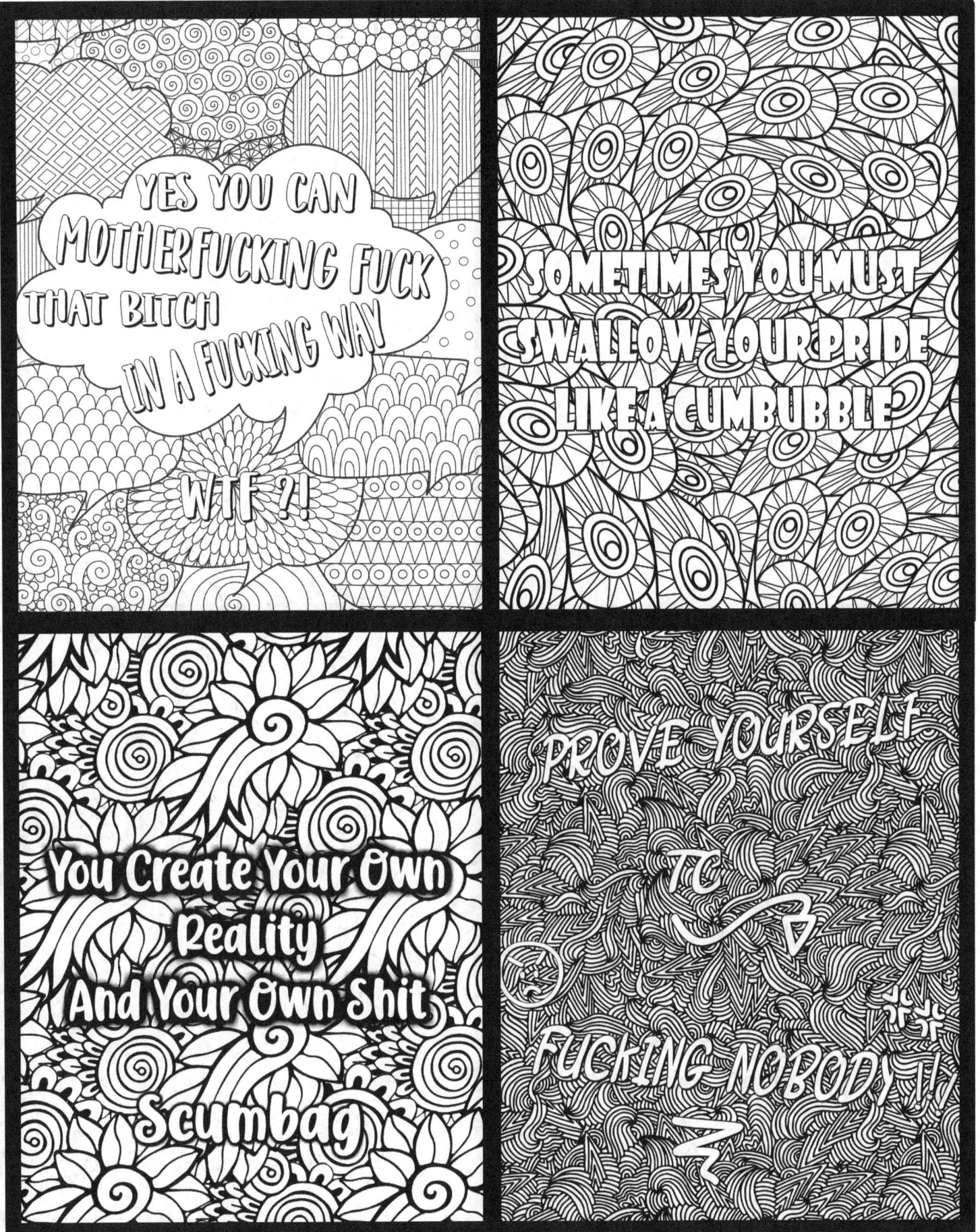

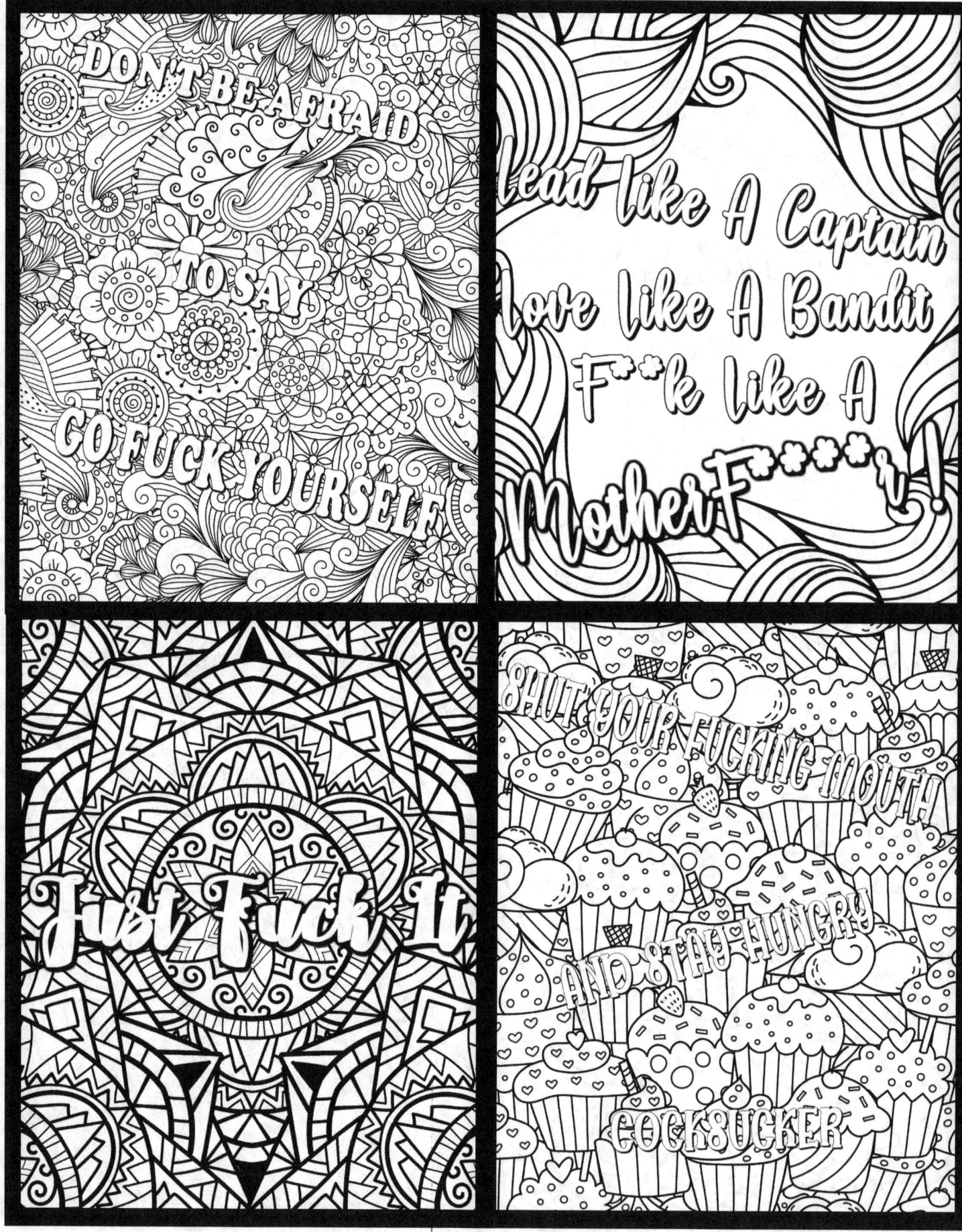

TEST YOUR PENCILS HERE

MORE TEST PAGES AT THE END OF THE BOOK

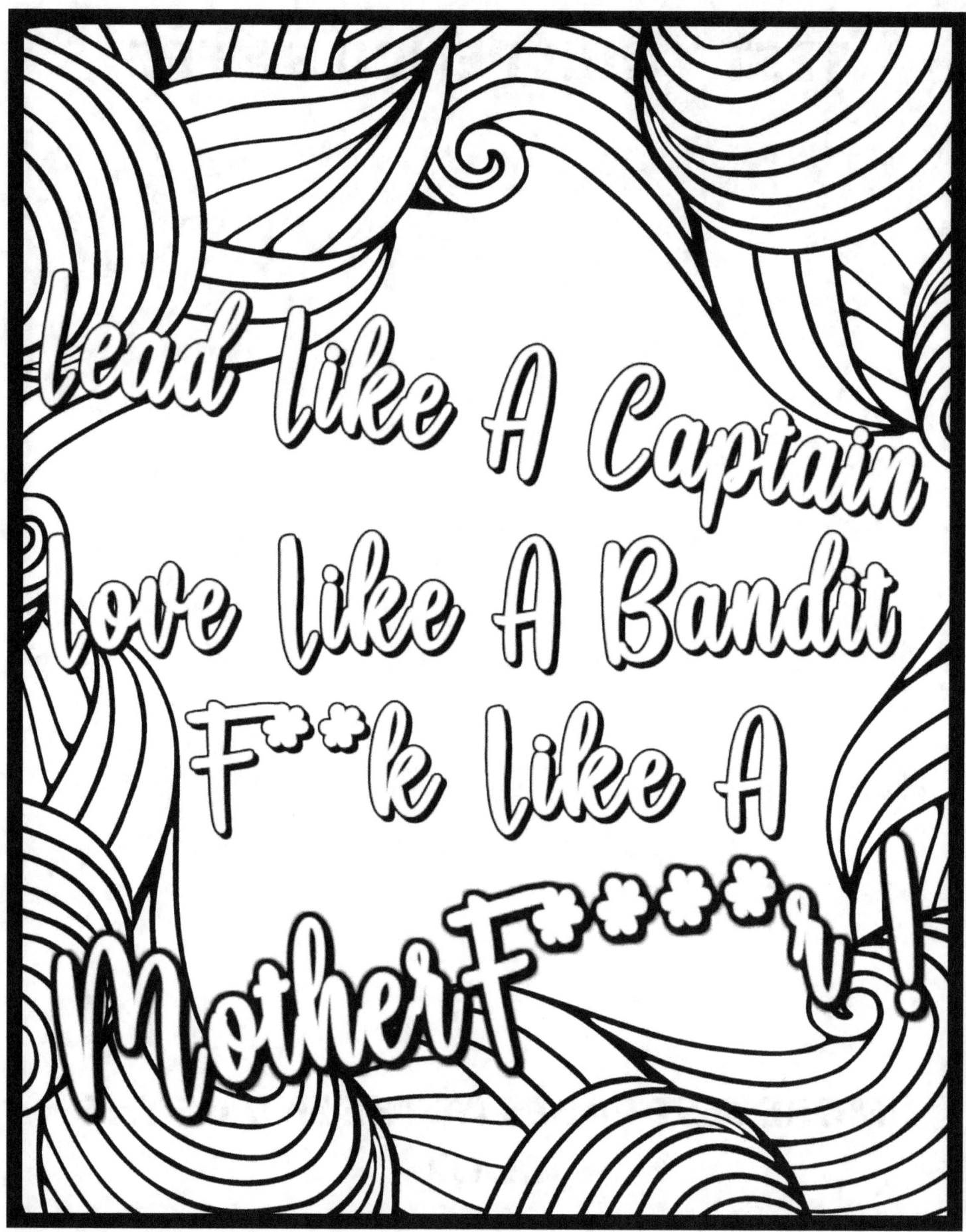

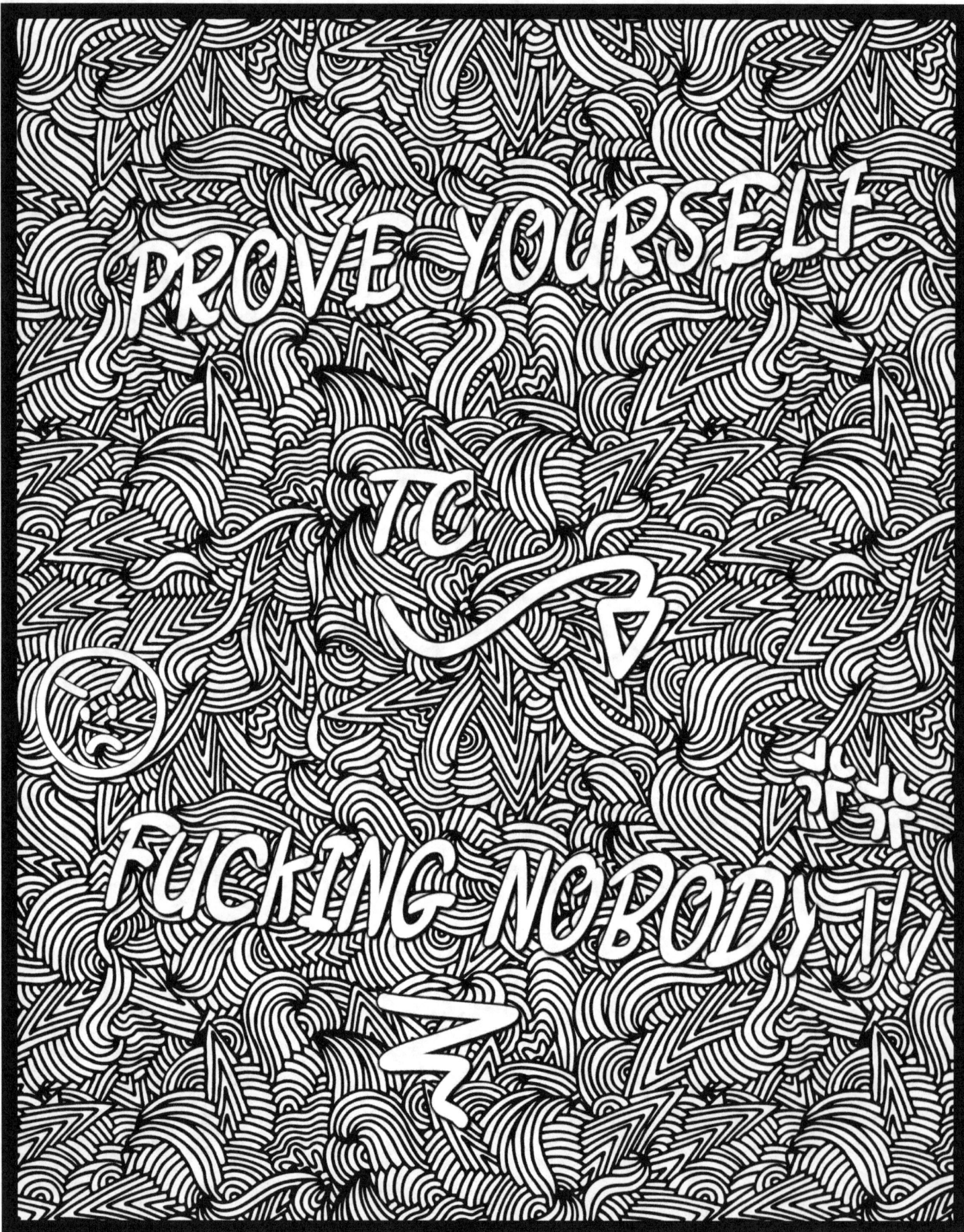

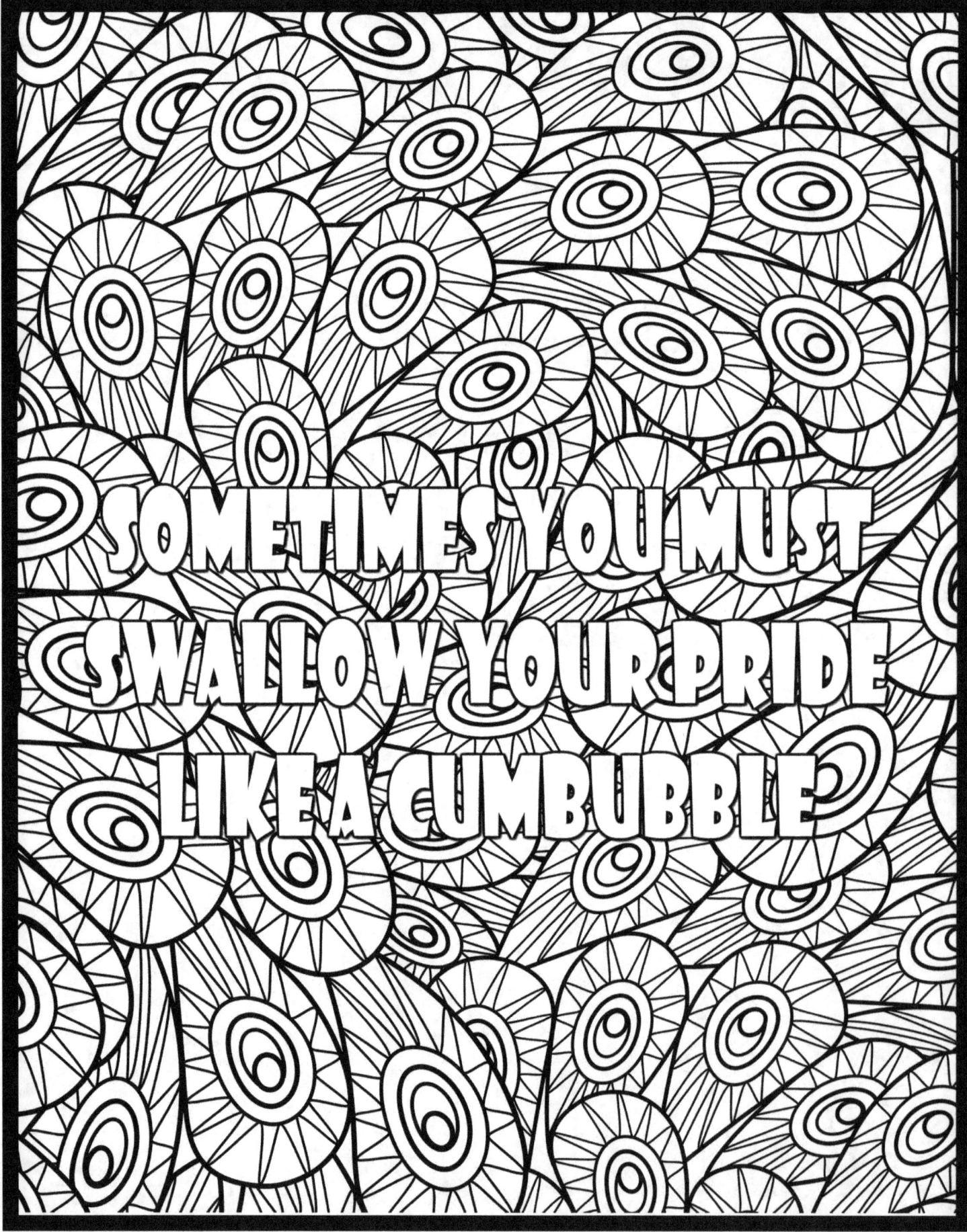

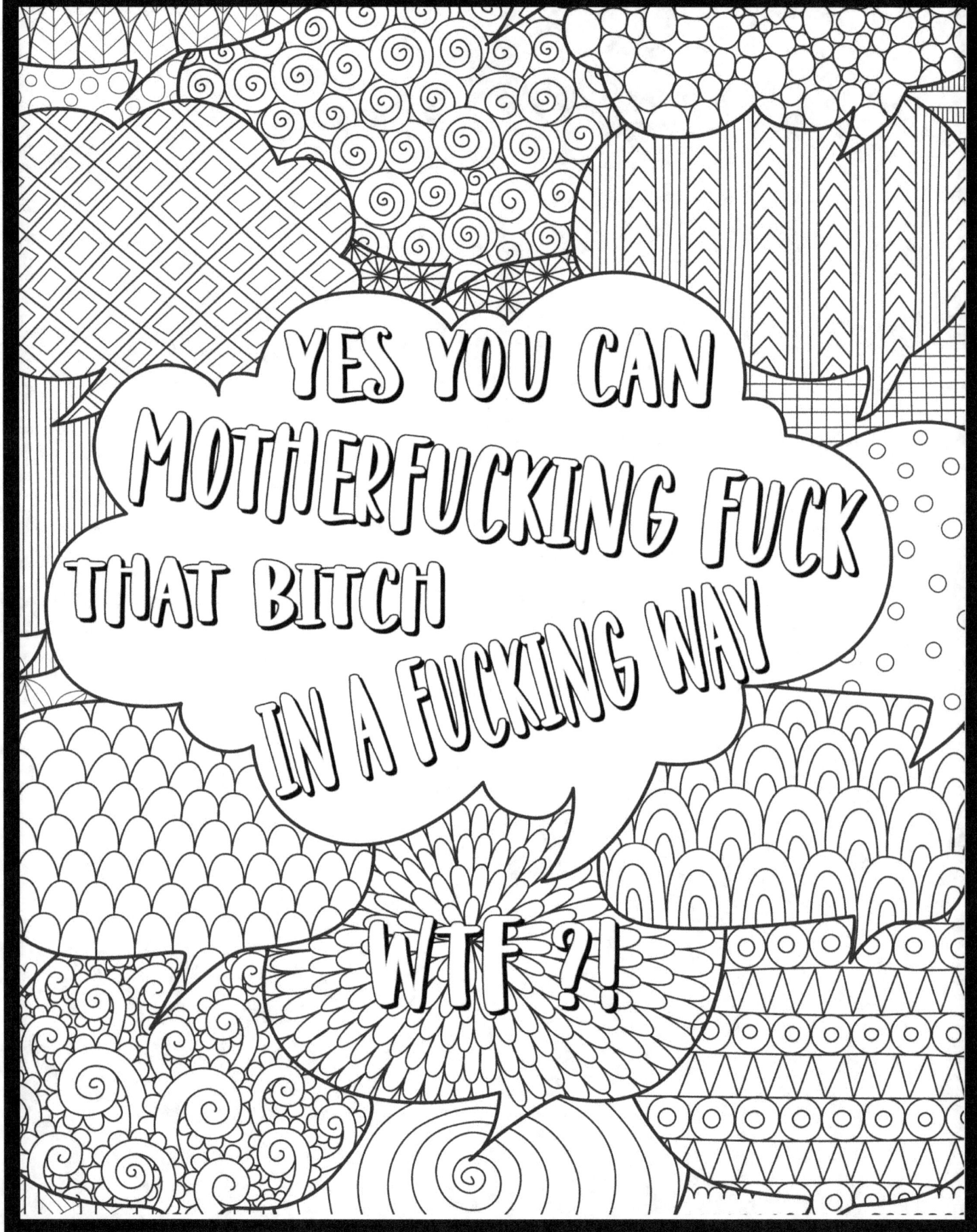

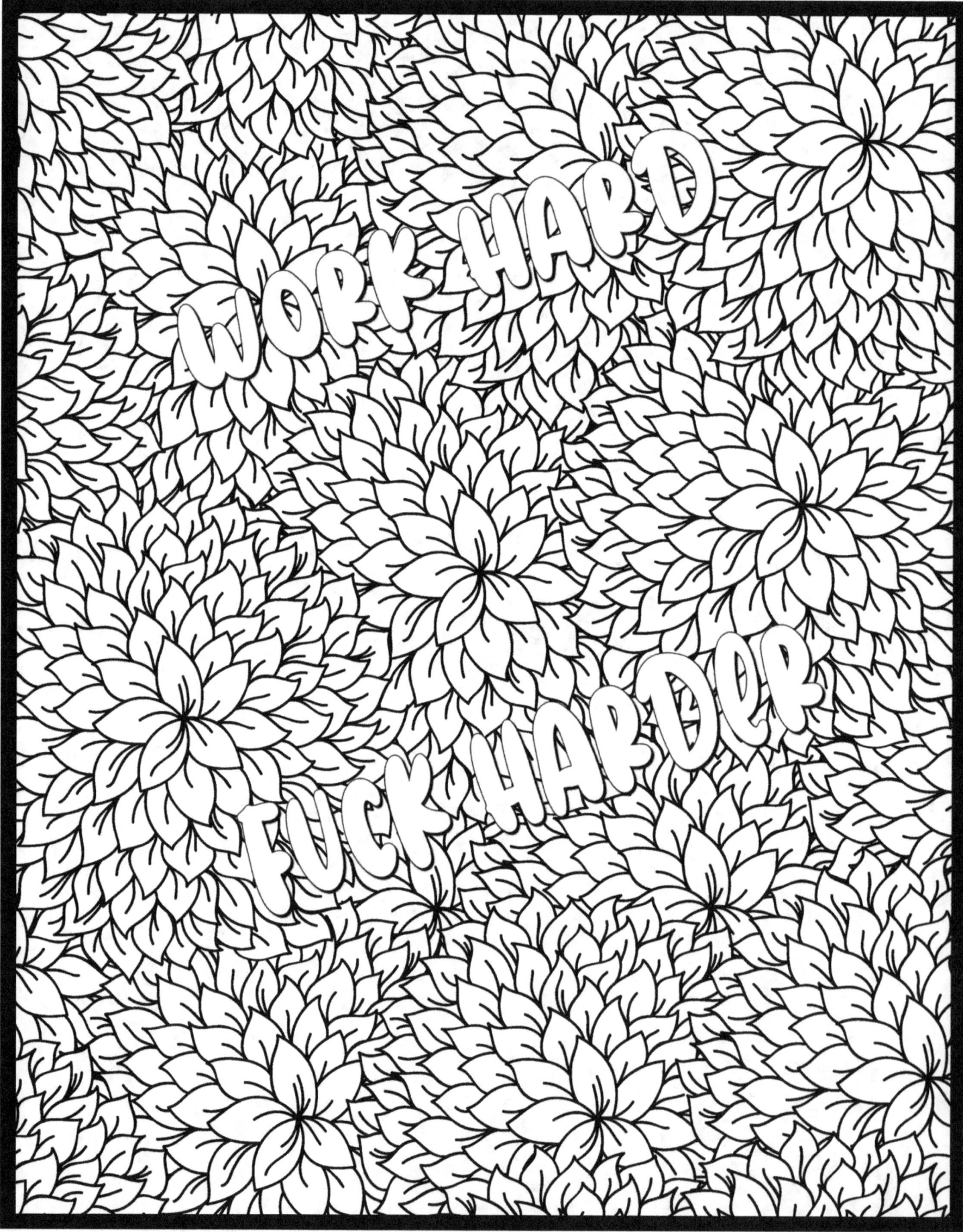

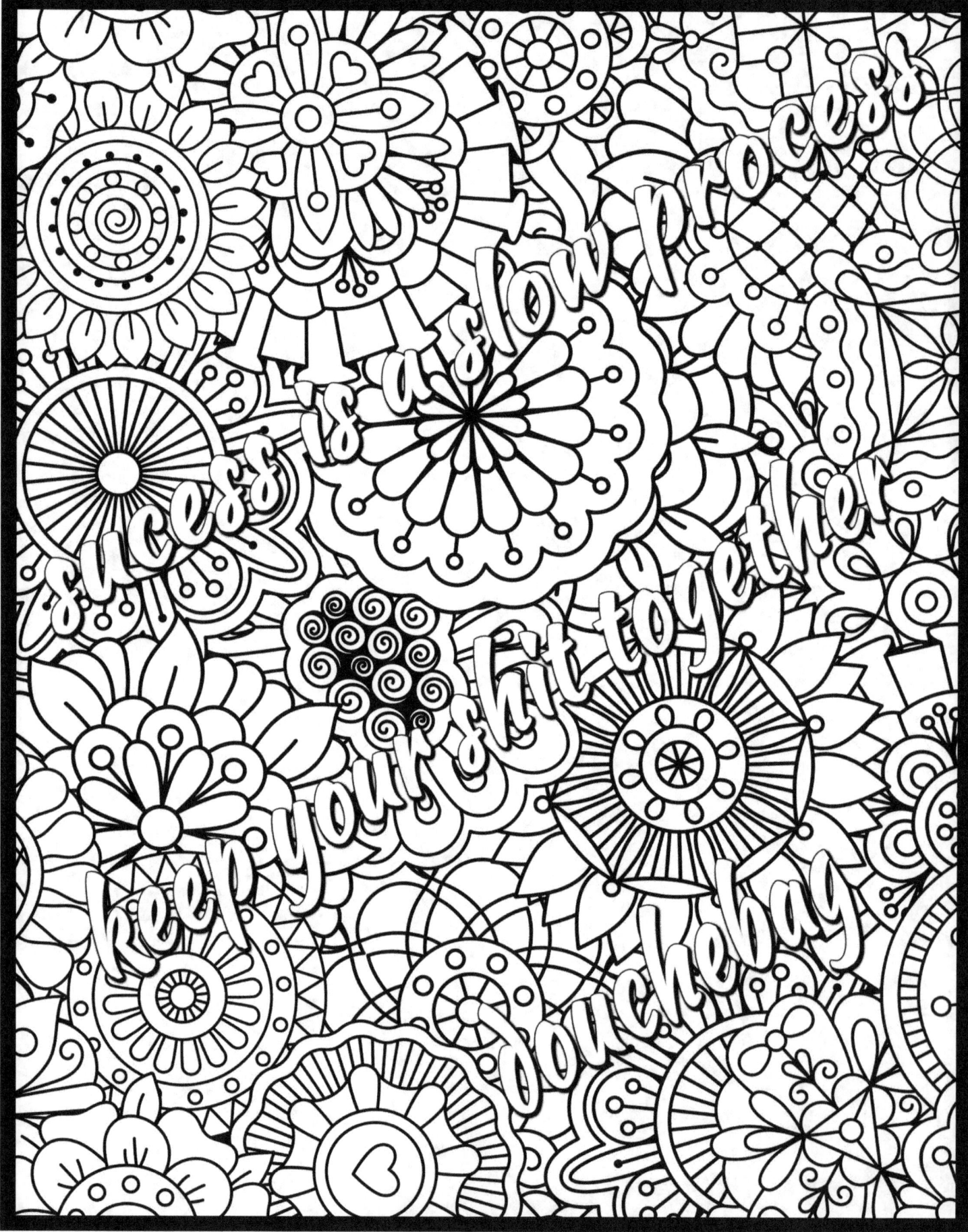

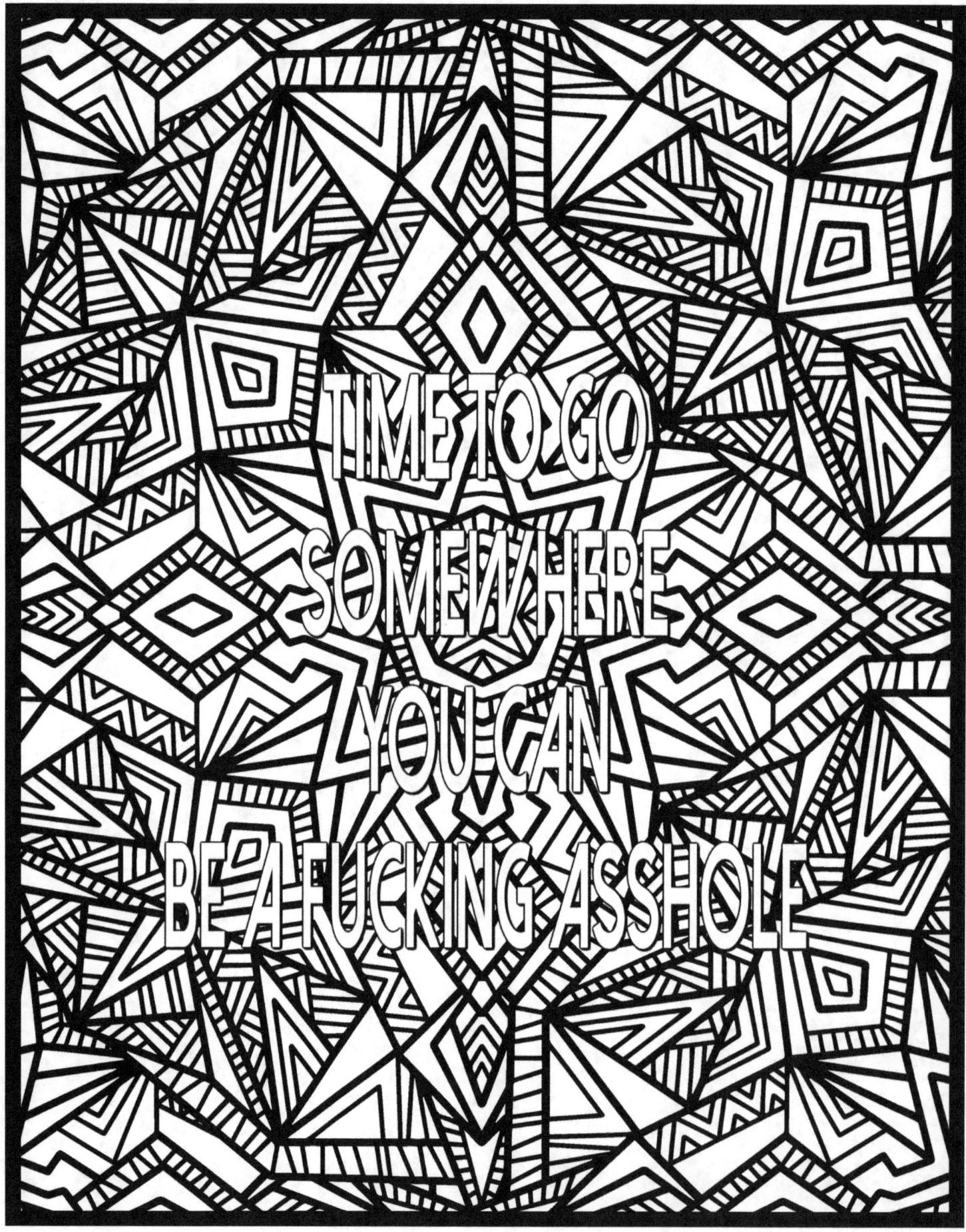

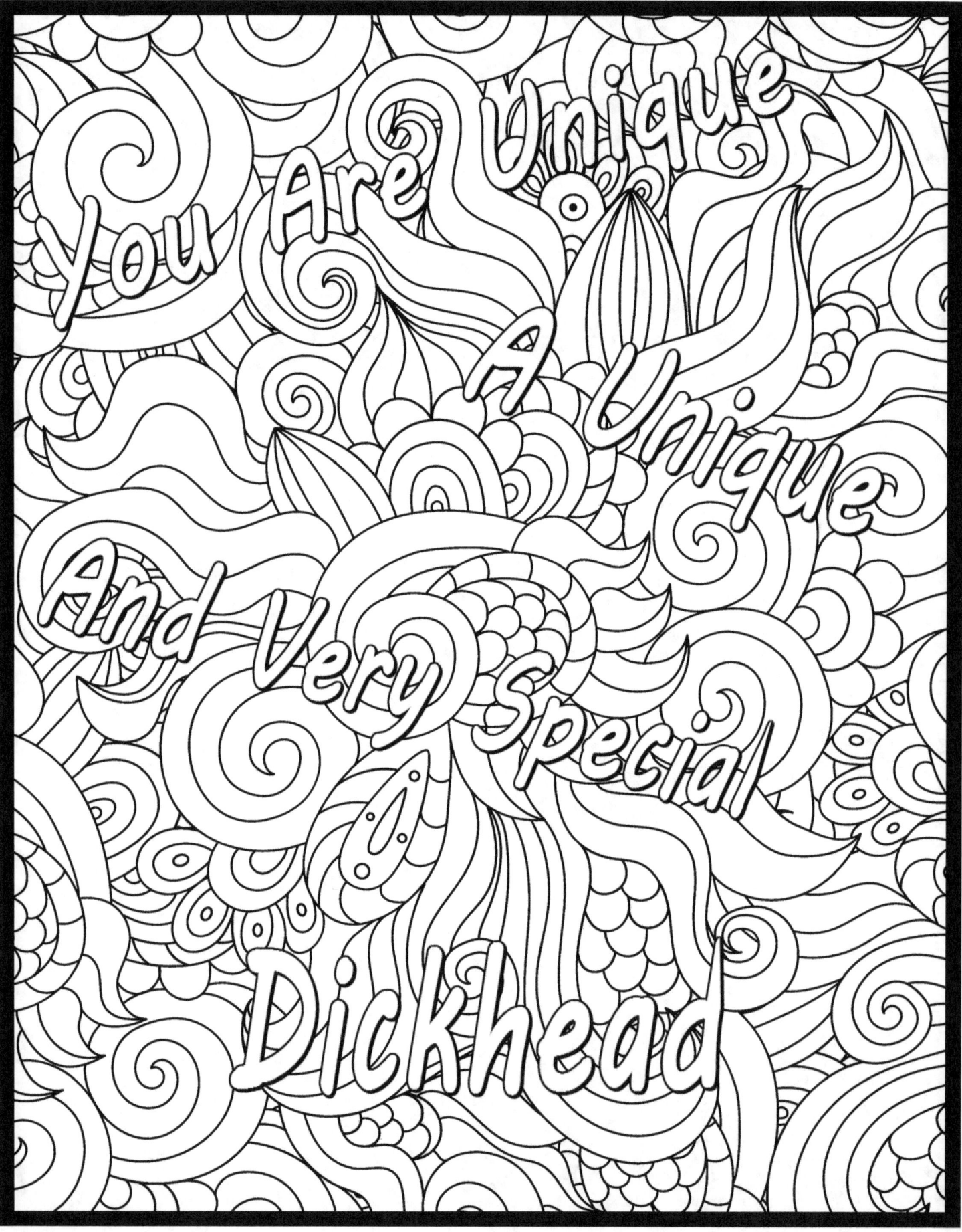

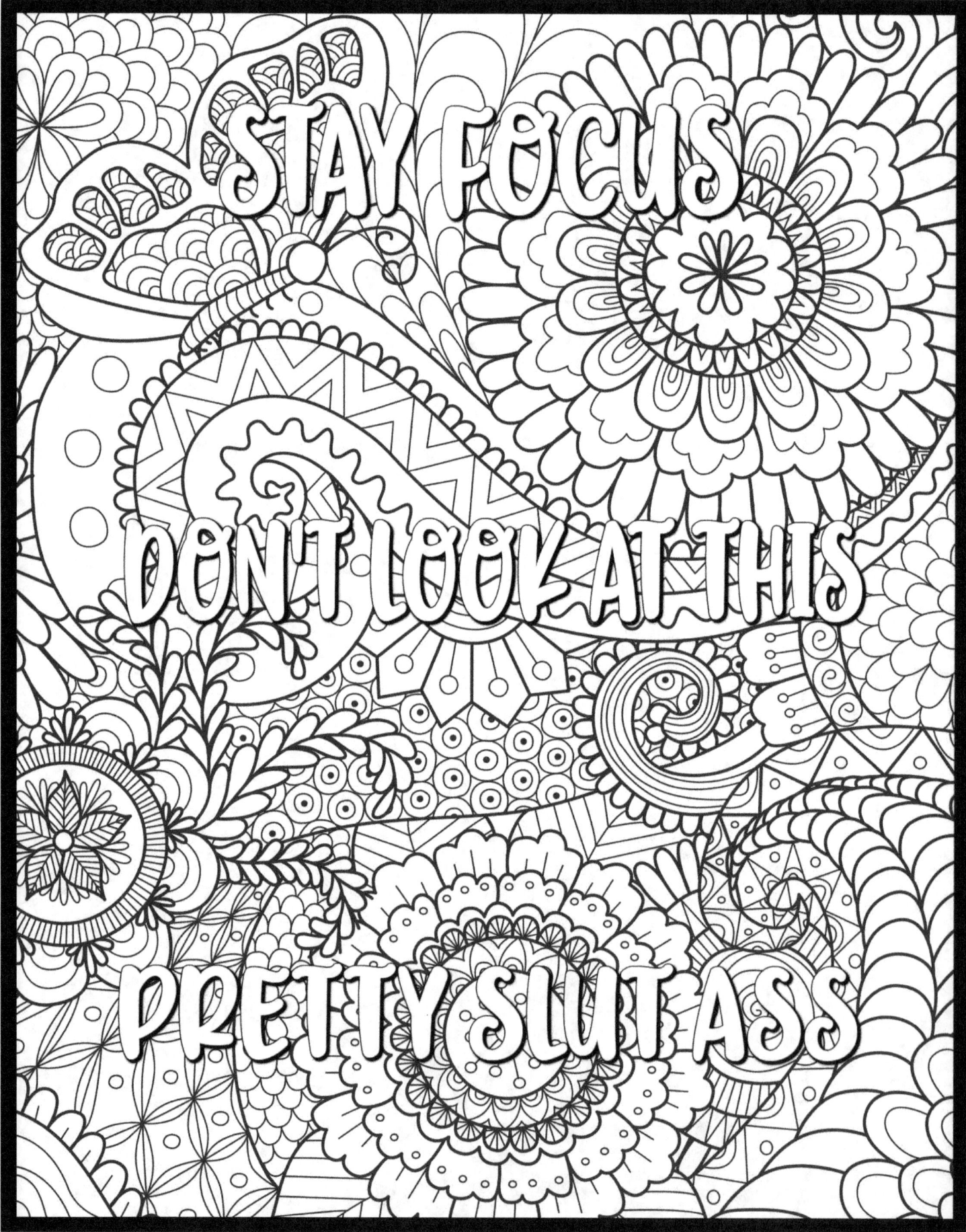

Don't Forget To Spread The Love

And Your AssWipe As Well

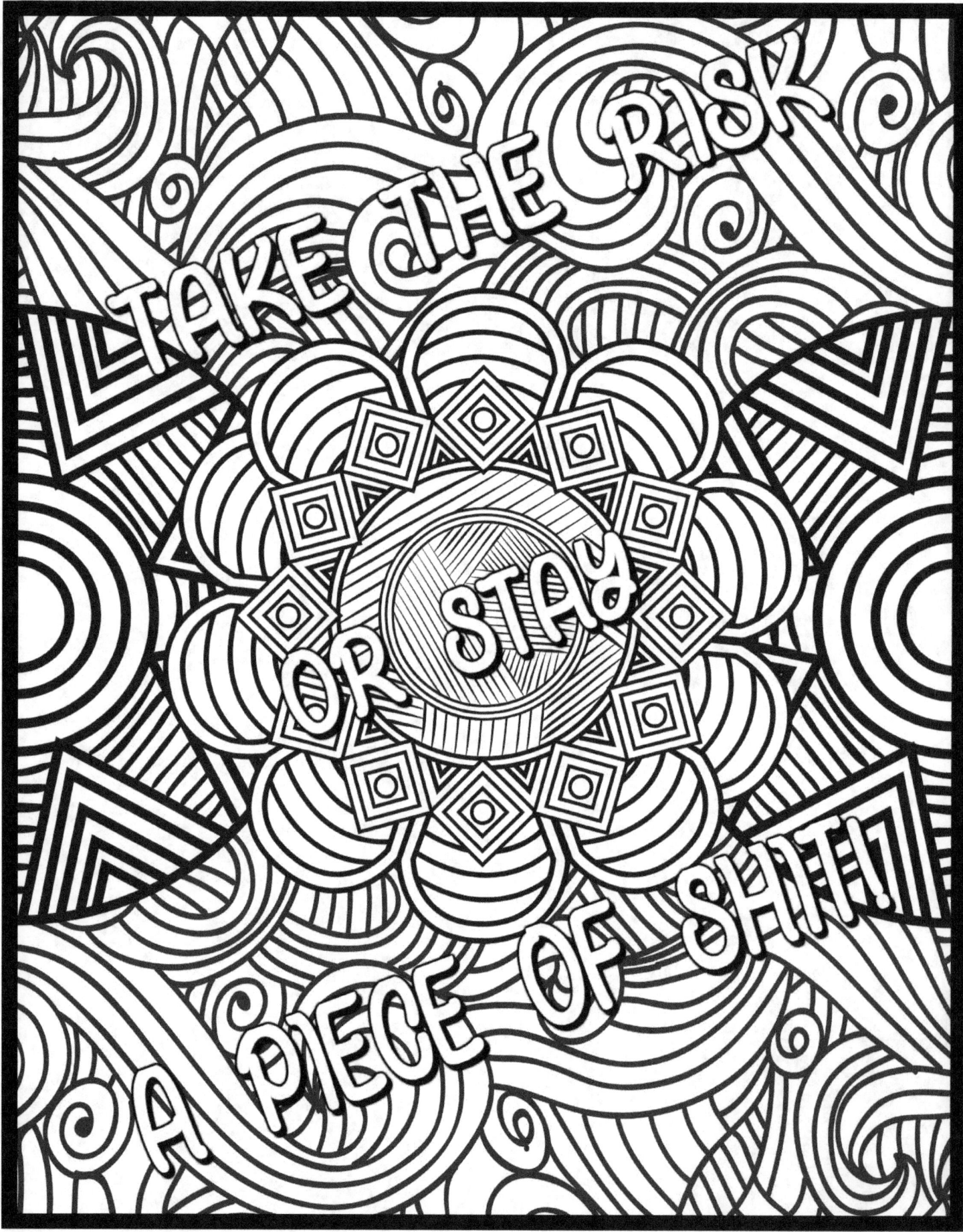

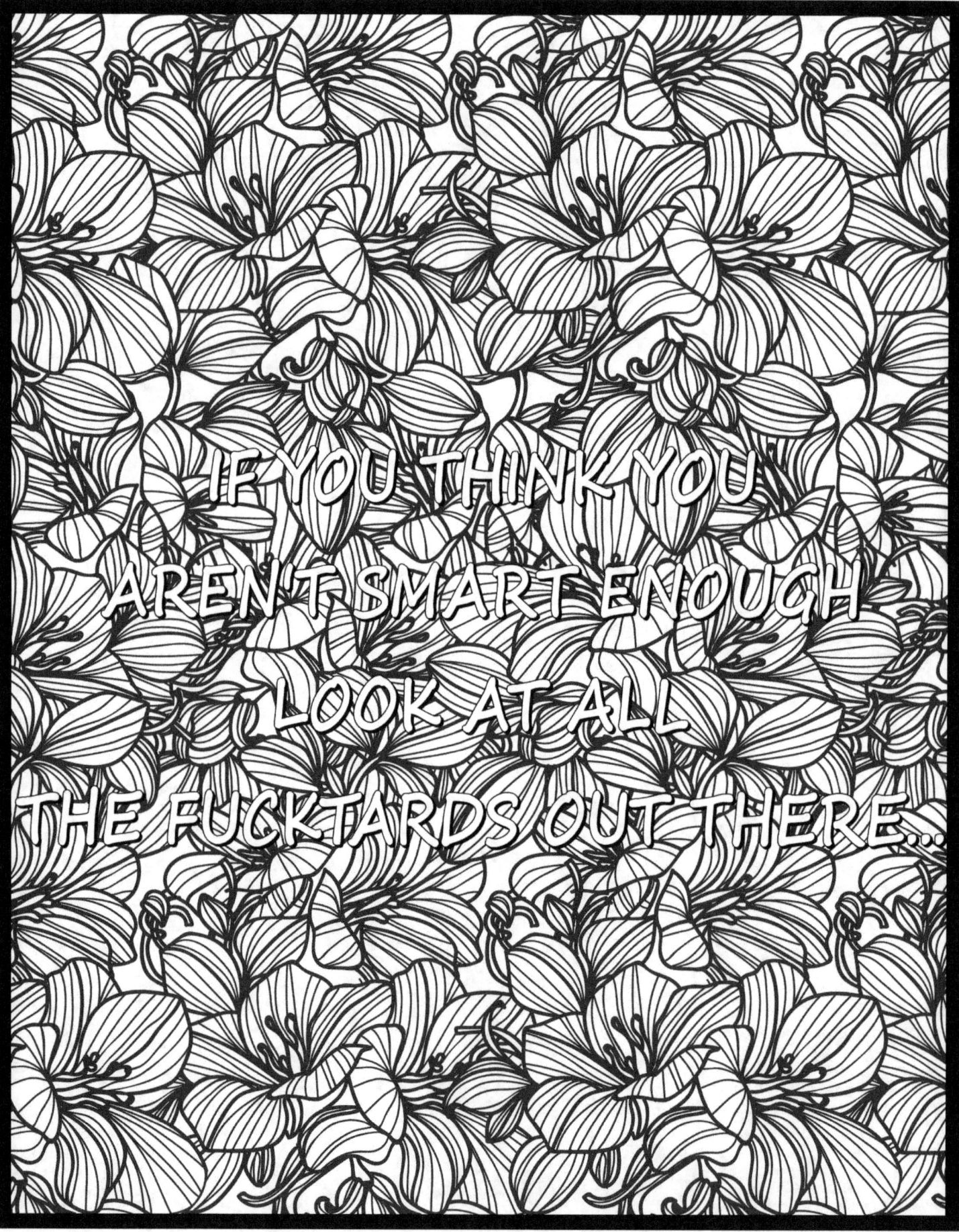

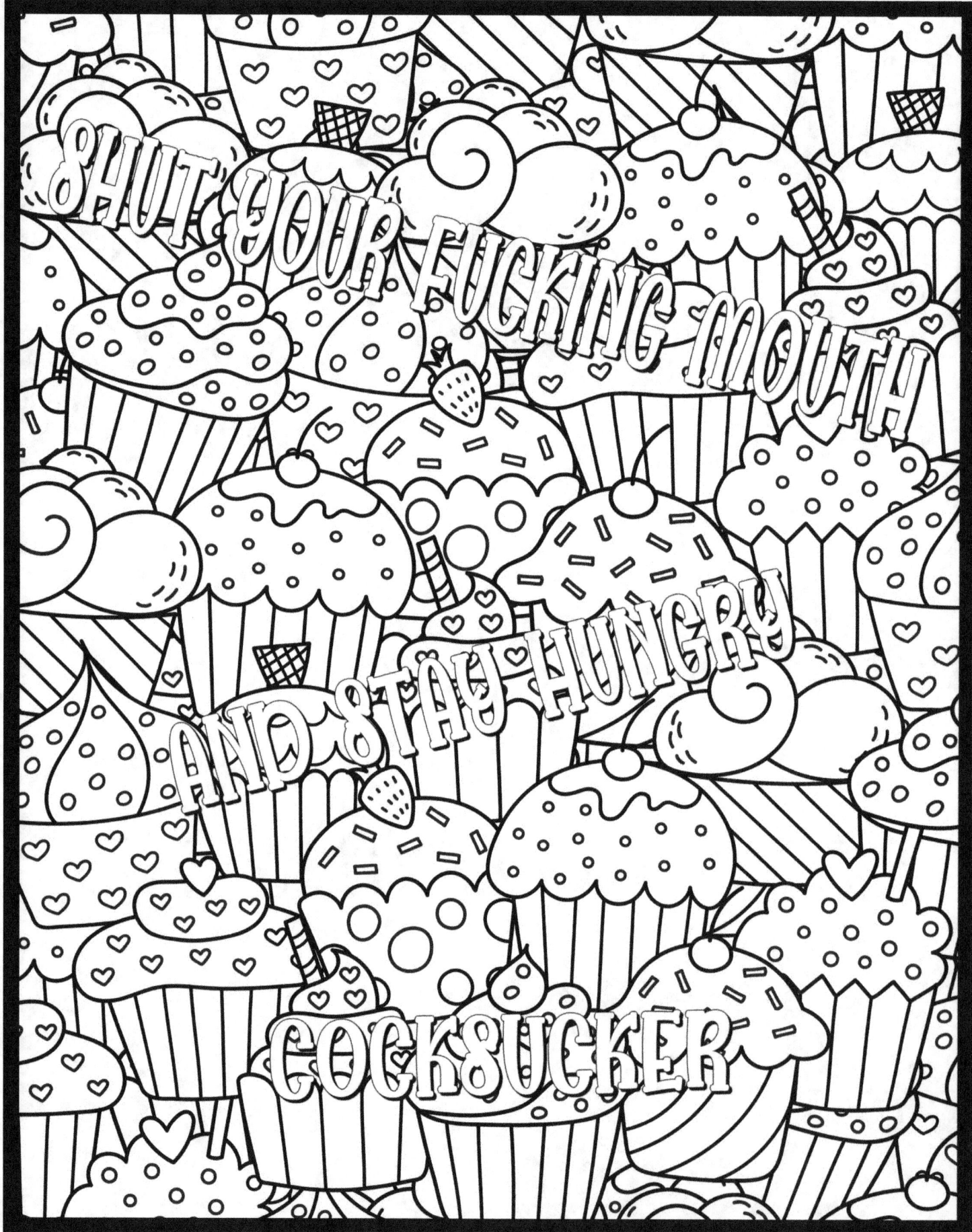

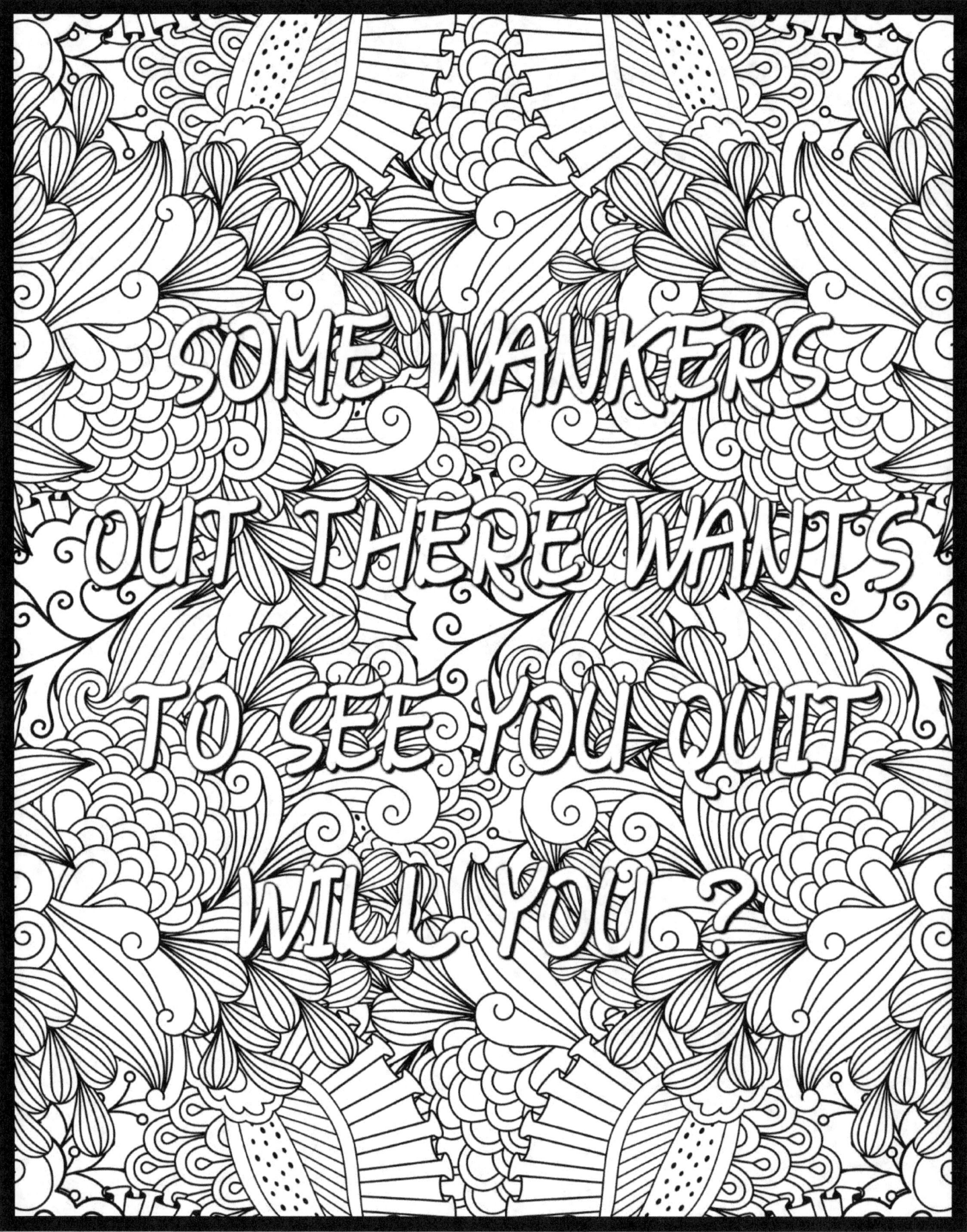

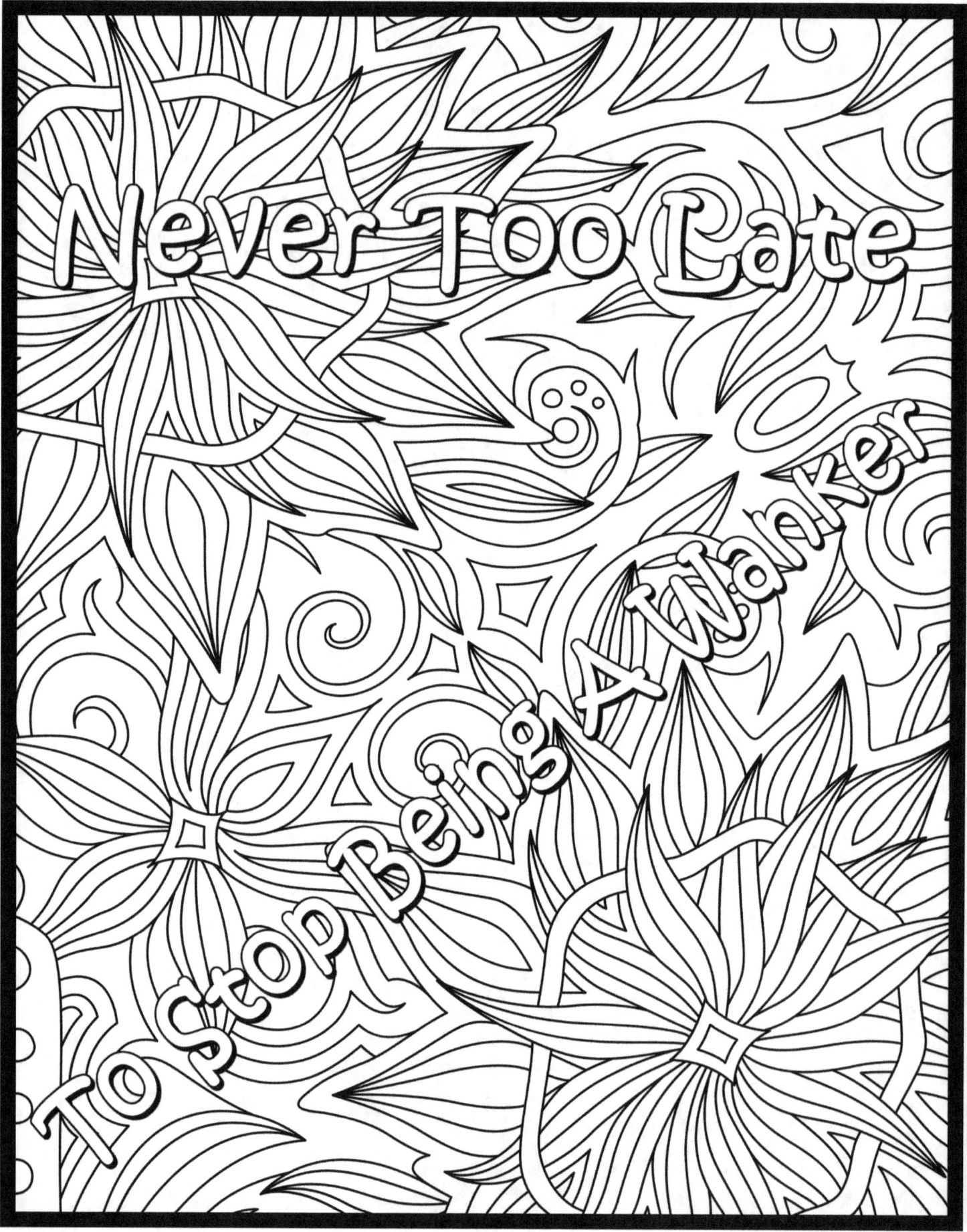

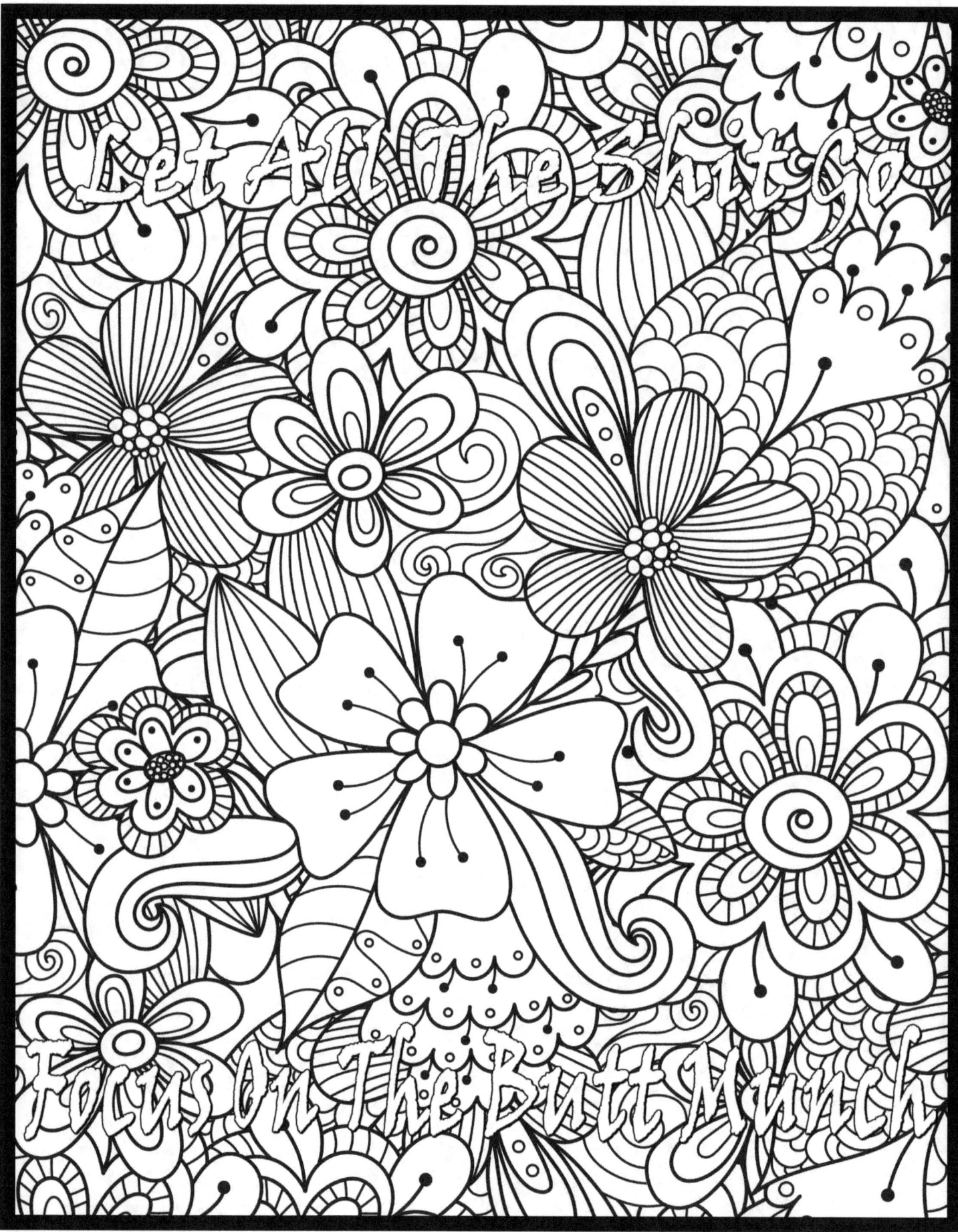

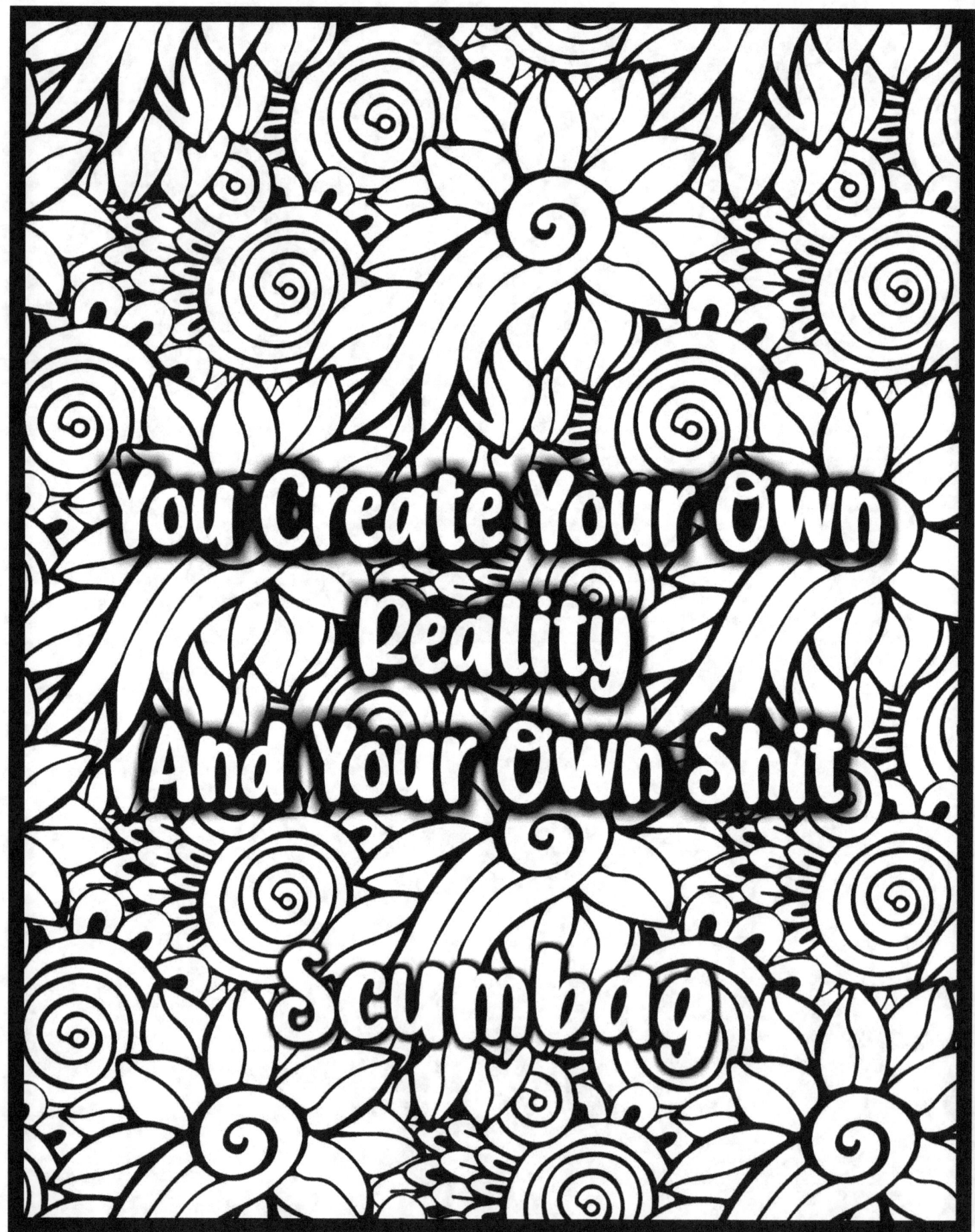

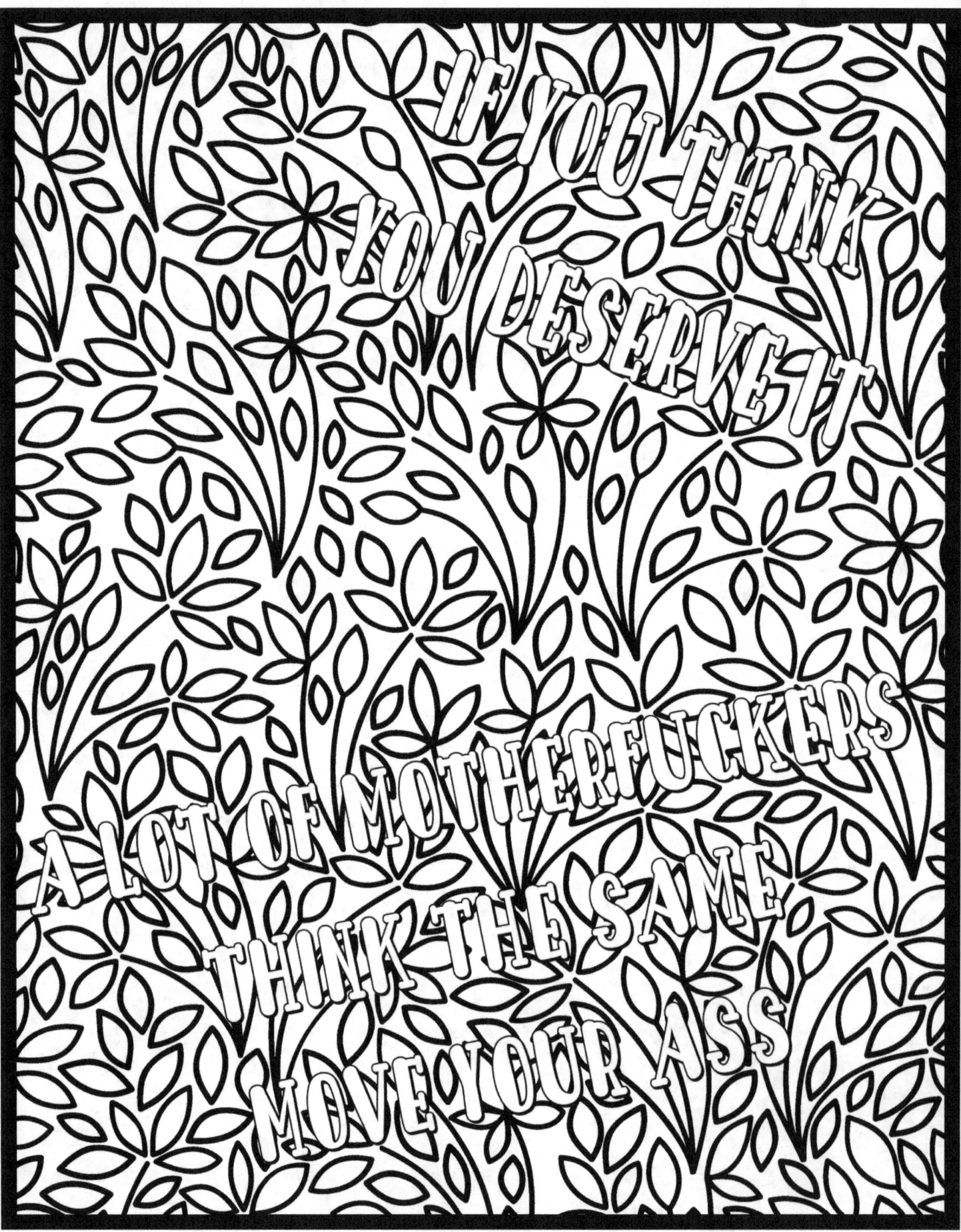

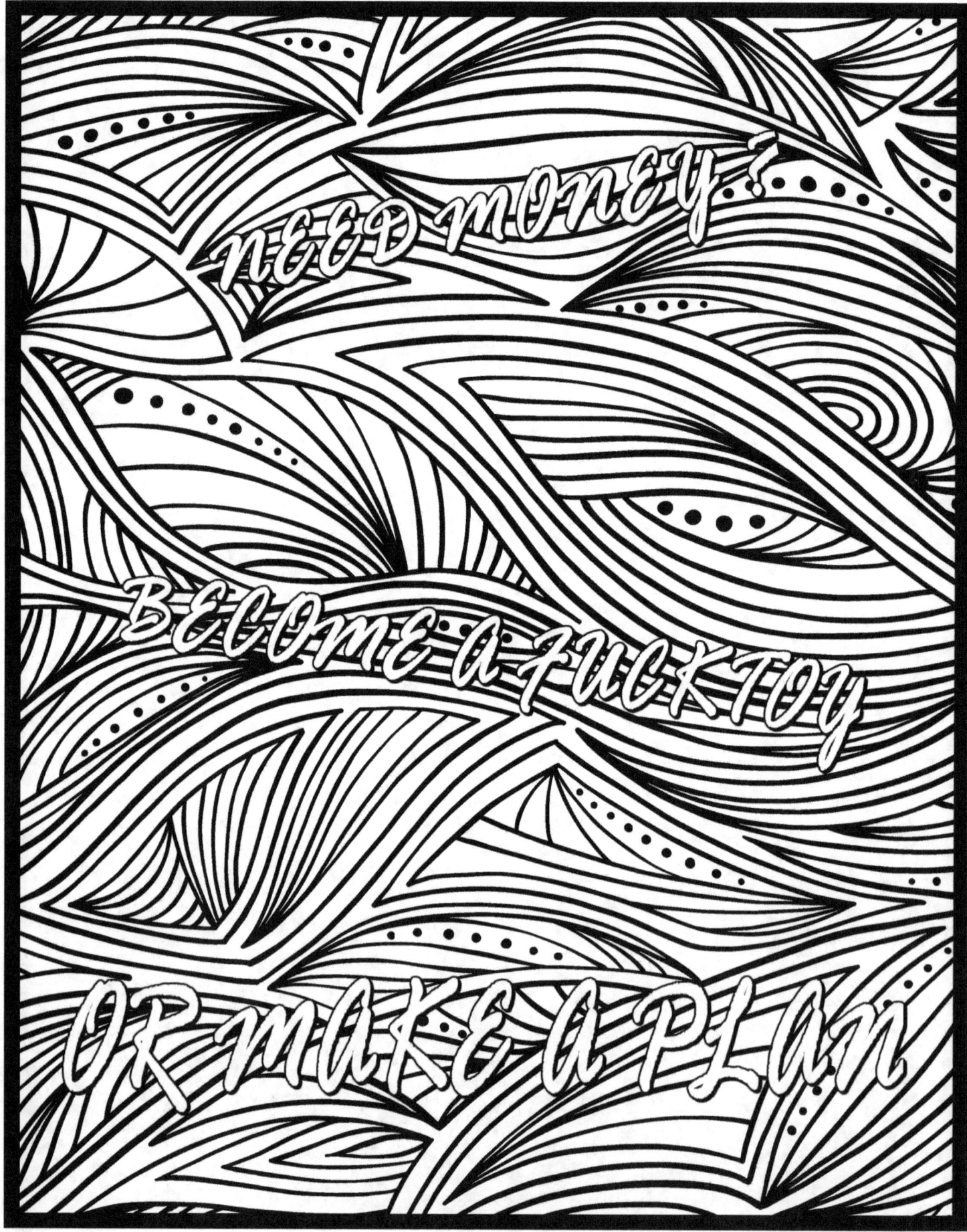

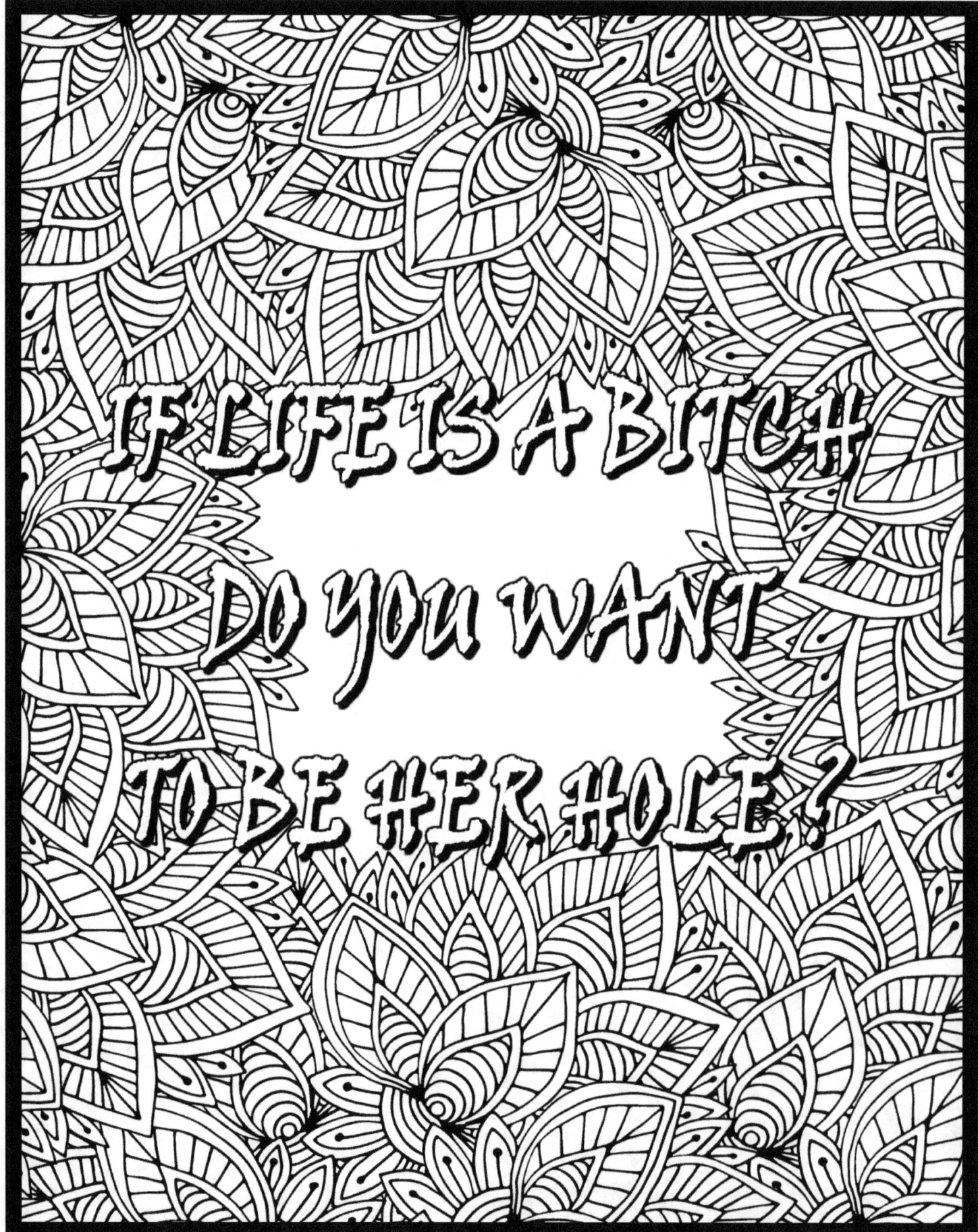

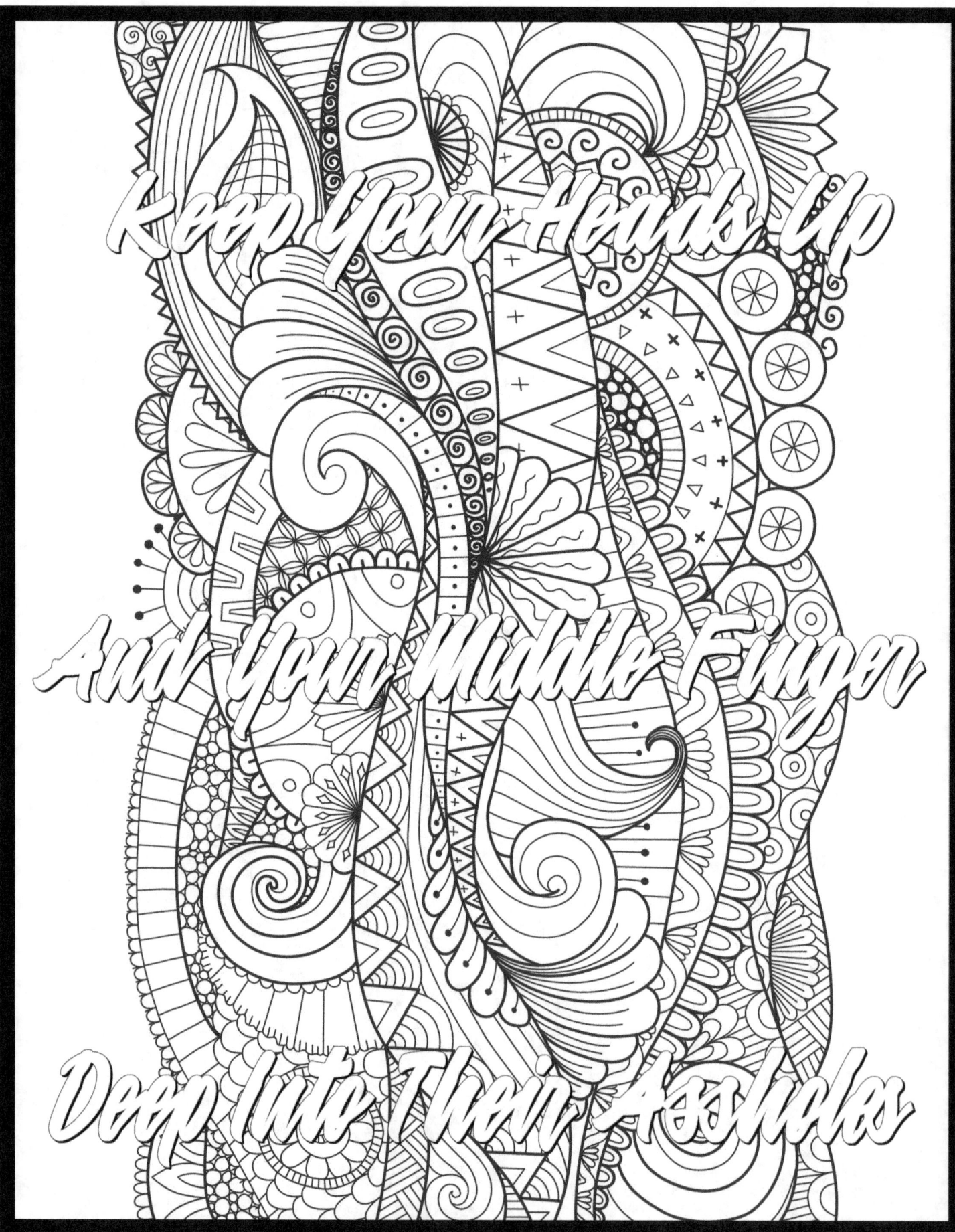

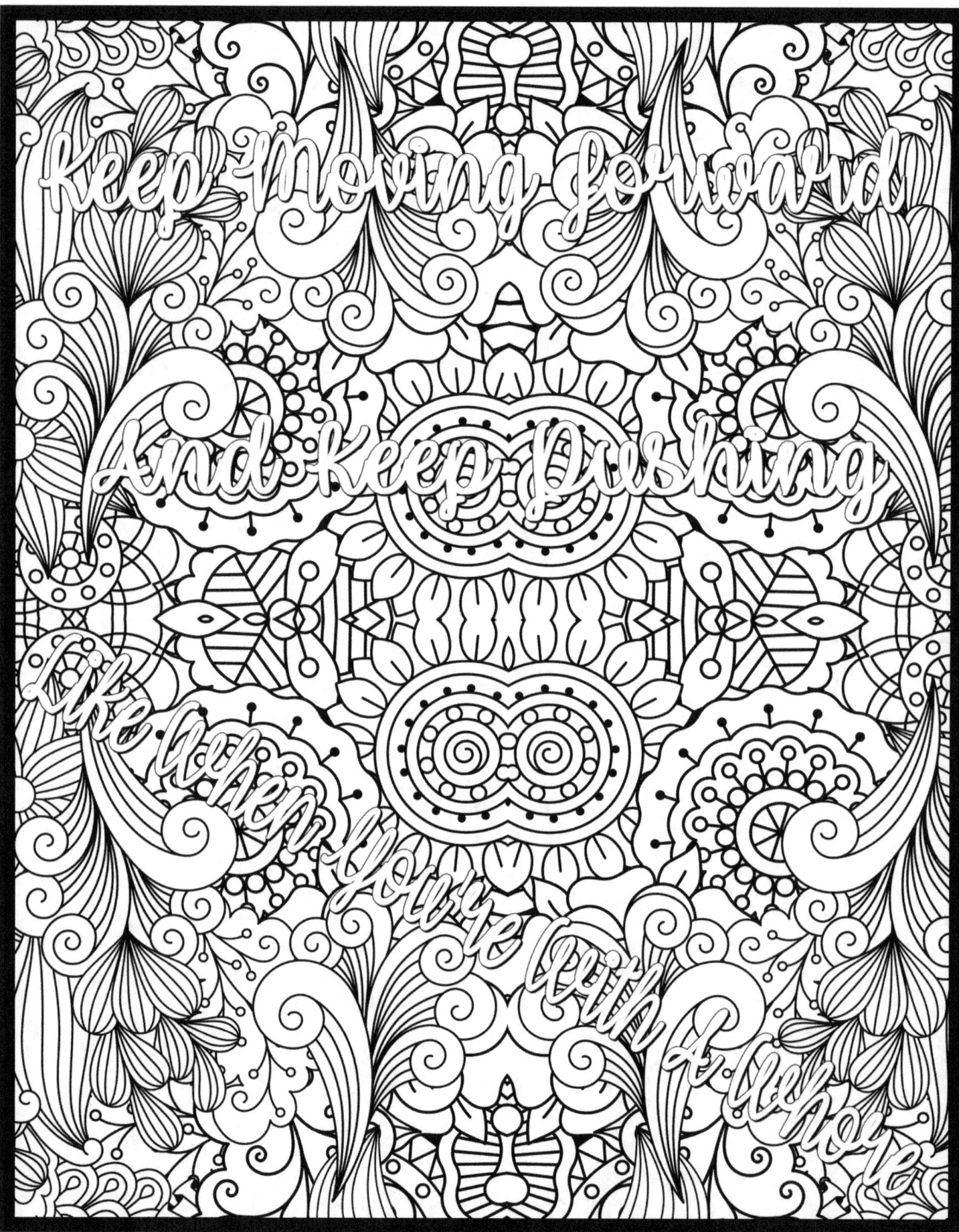

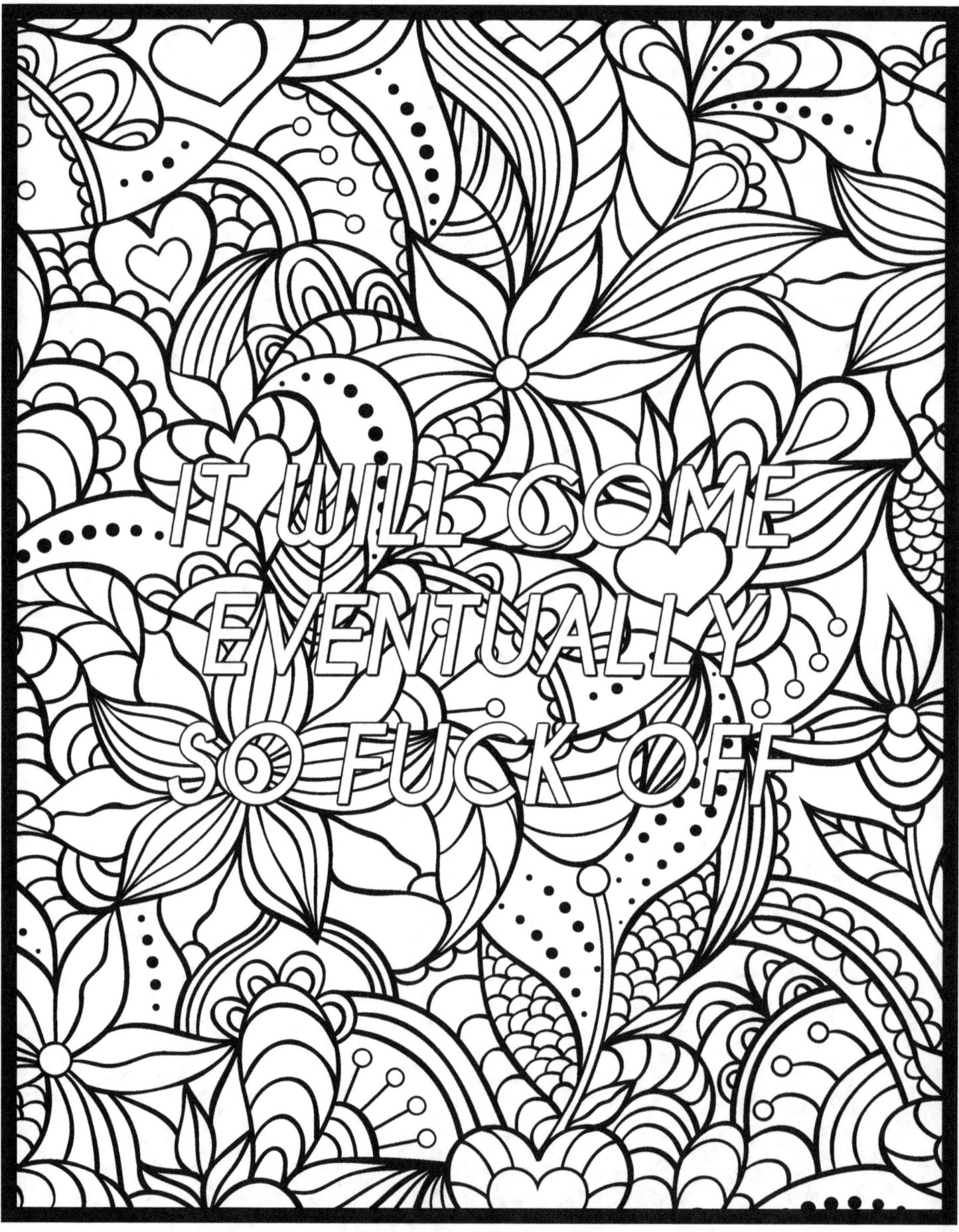

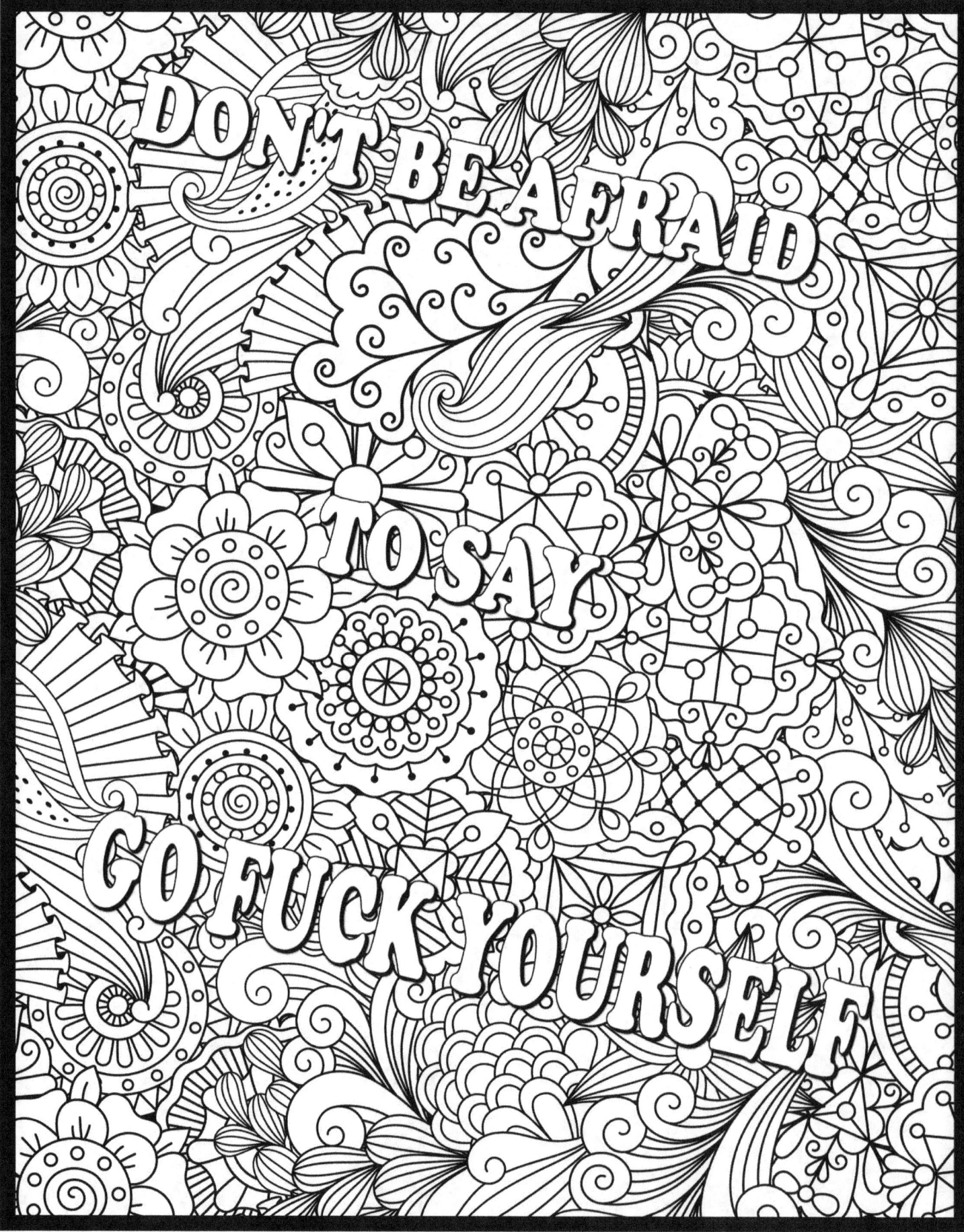

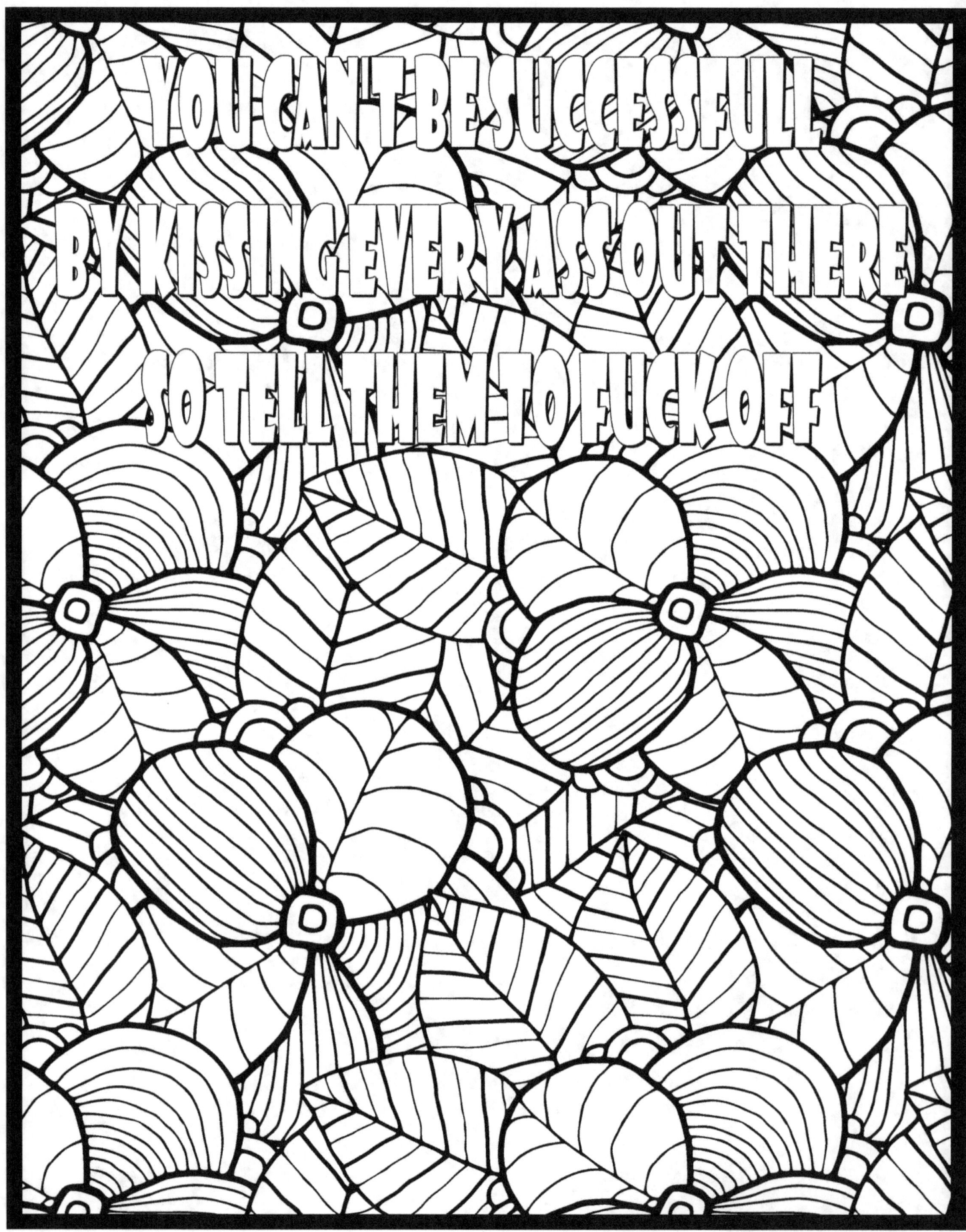

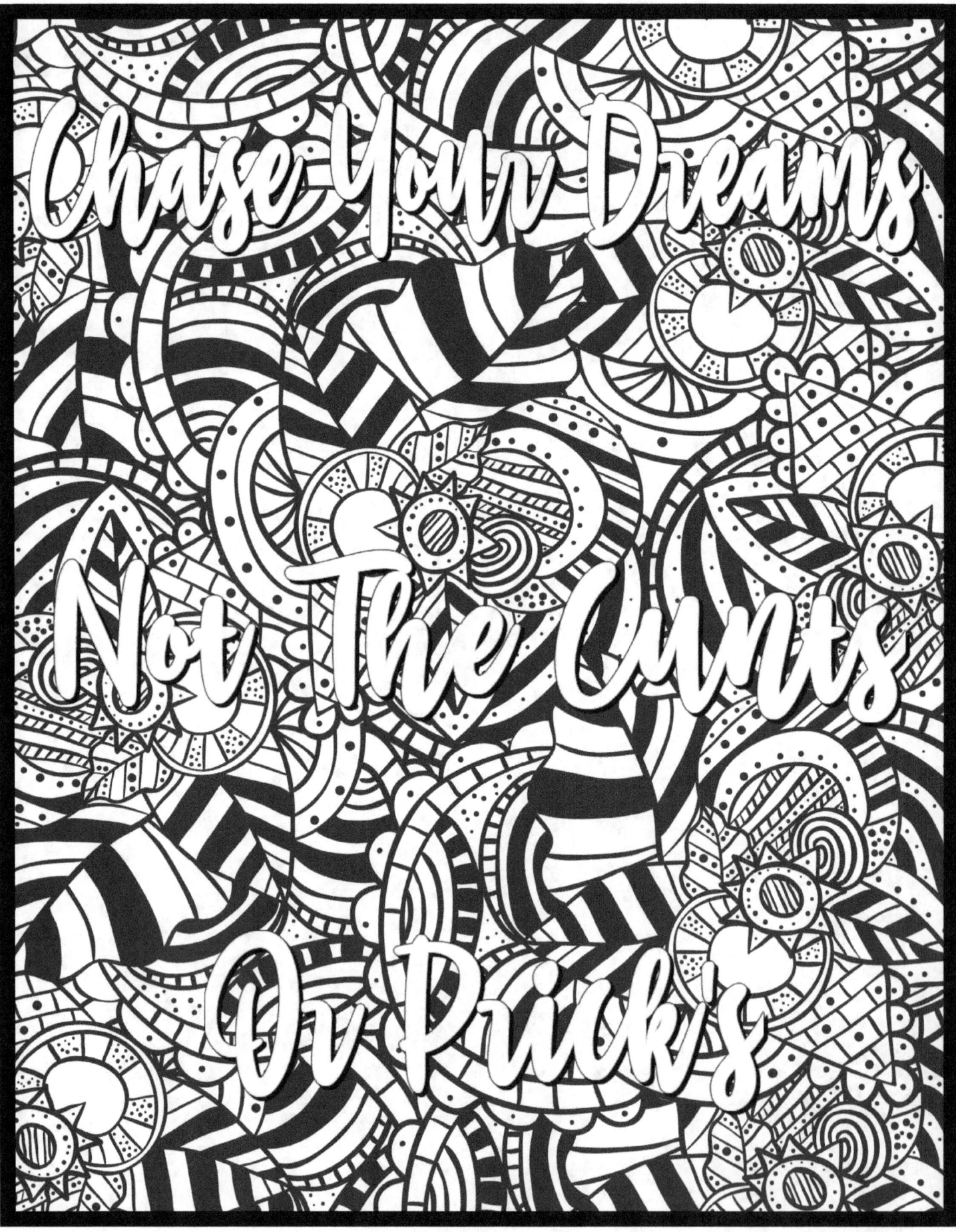

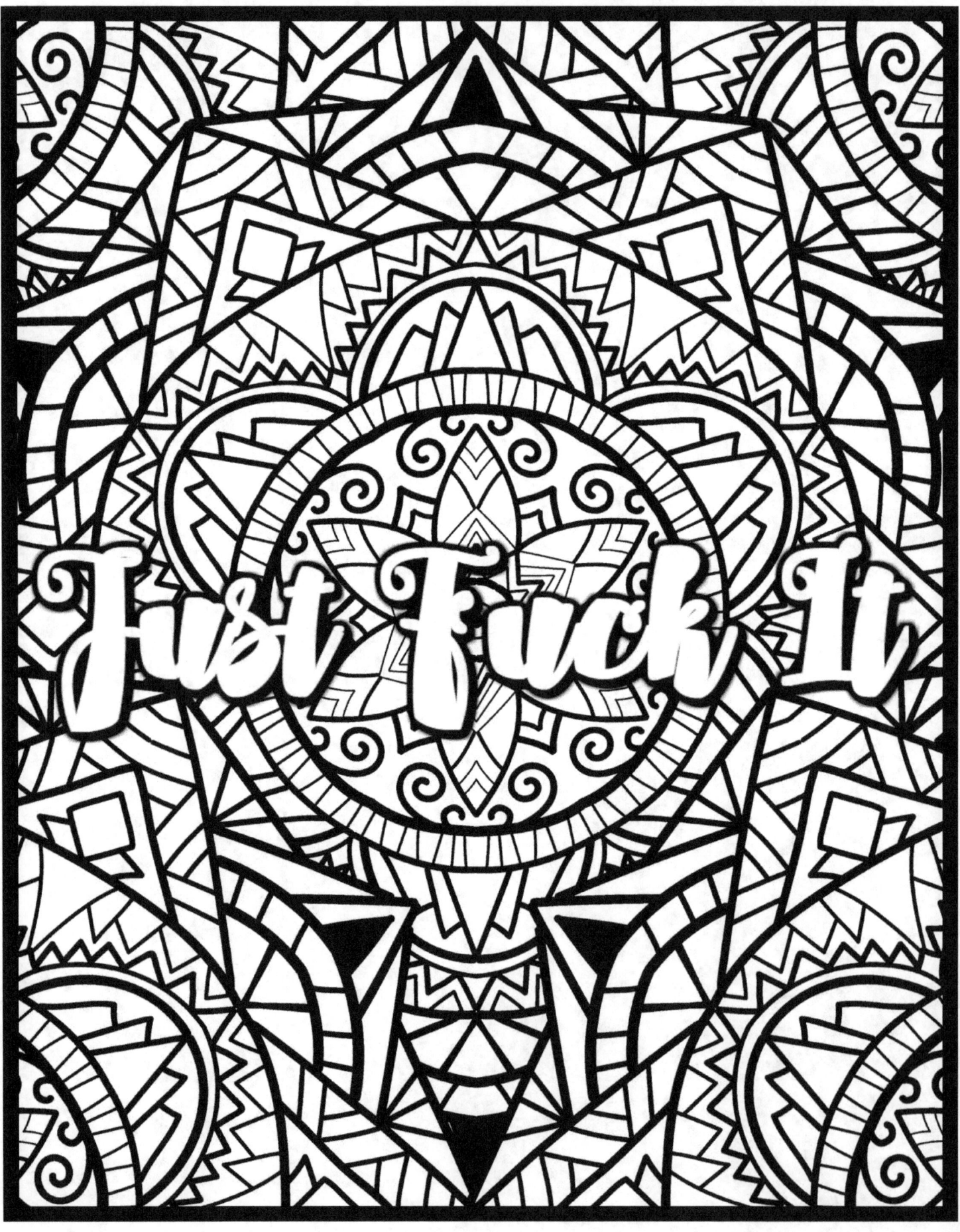

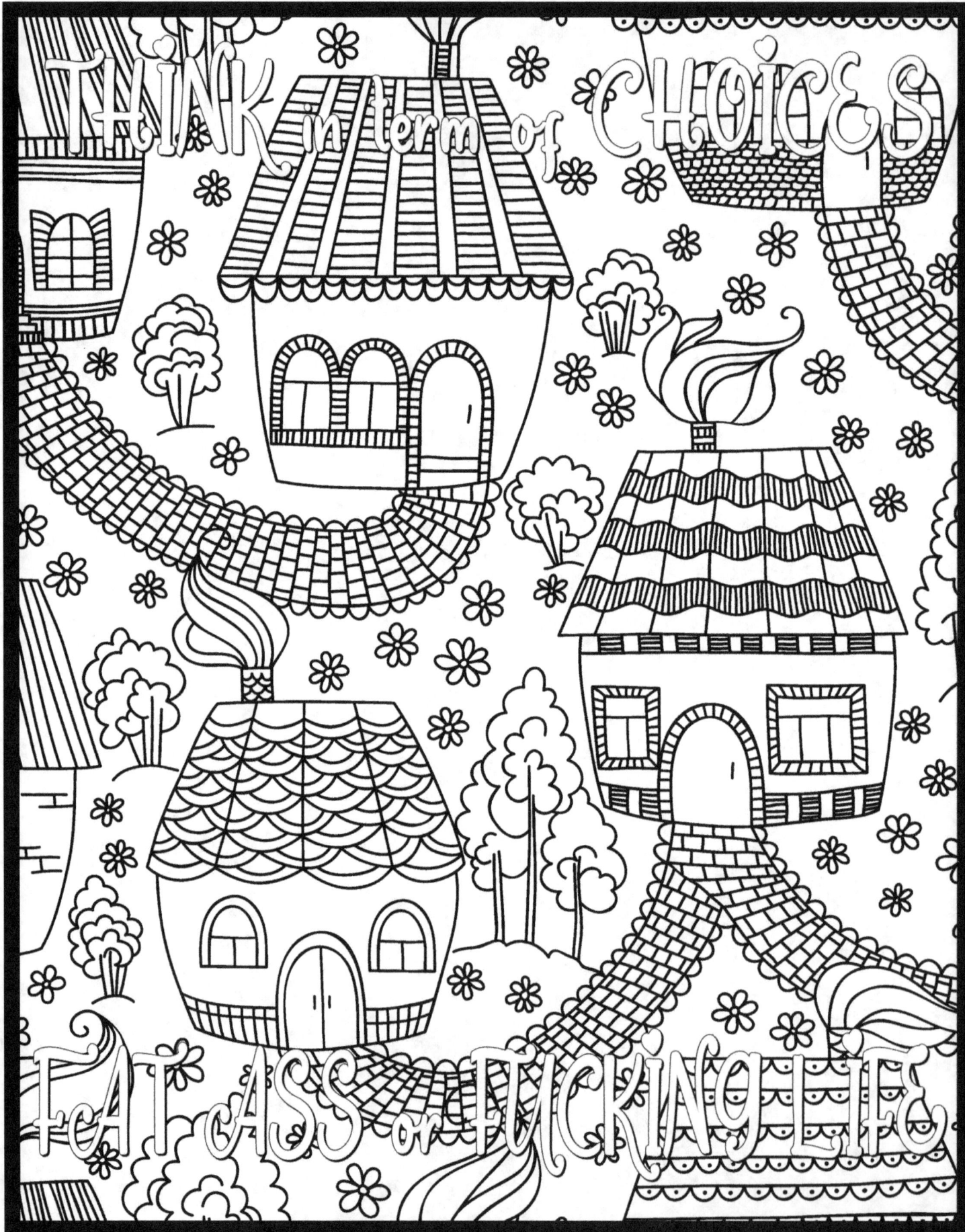

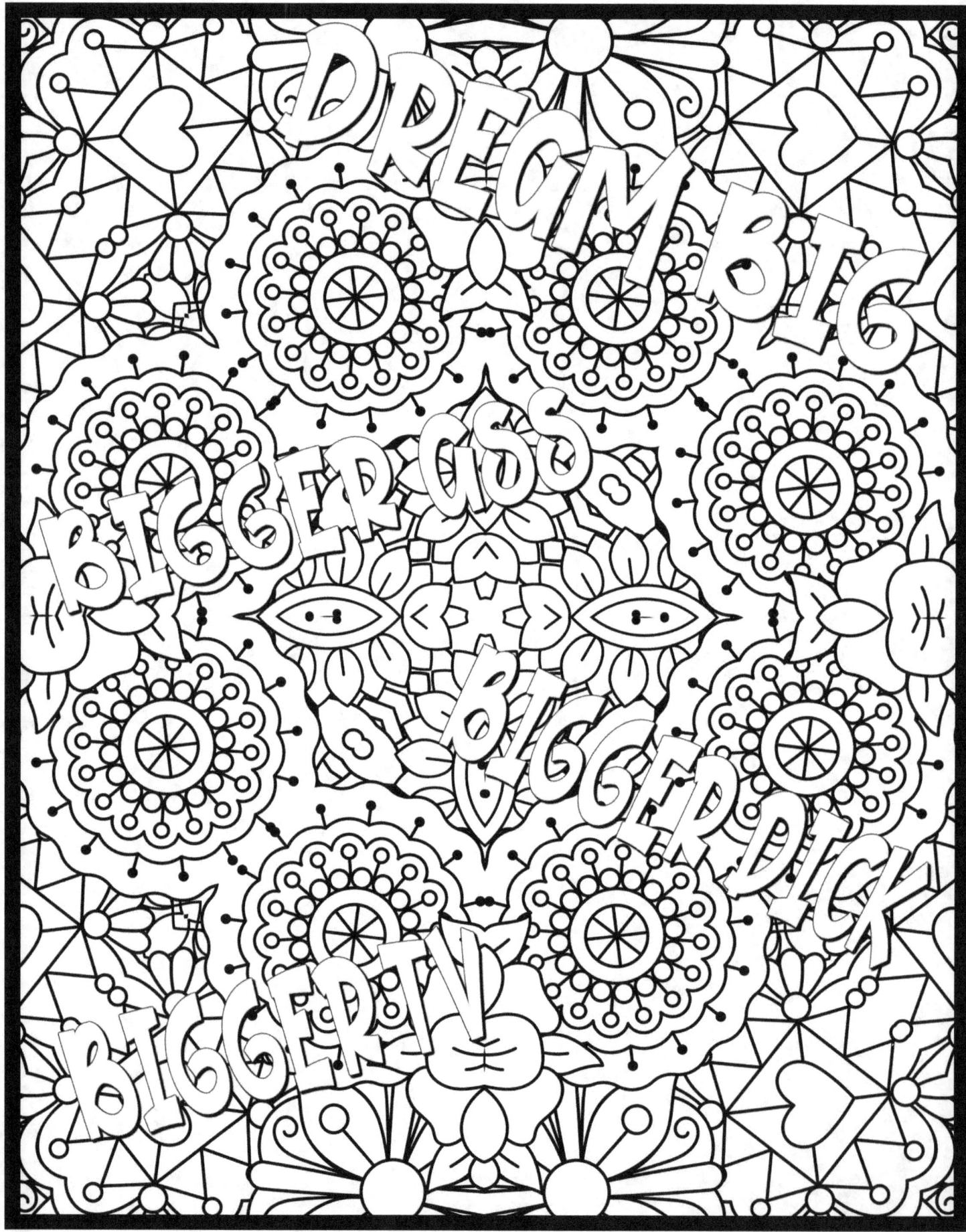

www.ingramcontent.com/pod-product-compliance
Lightning Source LLC
Chambersburg PA
CBHW080621220526
45466CB00010B/3414